KU-338-889

Insch, photographed about 1885, when it was shaped like a horse-shoe.
From Dr. G. Currie's "Annals of Insch".

HELLO, welcome to Insch. Perhaps you came to Insch from the south.

The wrought iron sign, half a mile from the village, was made by Mr. Sandy Simpson, a local blacksmith. Insch was created a Burgh of Barony by Mary Queen of Scots in 1565. The Queen's Baron was Andrew Leslie and included

within his barony was the village of Insch. At the annual fair of St. Michael, Andrew Leslie and his successors were given the power to choose bailies and officers. The bailies were commanded to make rules and regulations for "the advantage of the said burgh" and bring to the Barony Court and administer penalties on those who did not conform. The bailies were also allowed to create freemen of the burgh who were given the privilege of brewing, baking and selling food and other necessities freely. The people of Insch could hold a market every Sunday and two free fairs yearly on St. James' Day, 24th July and St. Drostan's Day, 14th December.

"The name Insch is generally considered to be of Celtic origin and to signify an island. It is not improbable that the Insch had originally been confined to the small town or village in which the church stands, or, at all events, to the spot of ground which forms the site of the village, which bears some marks of having been at one time surrounded by water". (The 1842 Statistical Account.)

The beds of old streams, I have been told, run beneath some older houses in Insch. The streams having been diverted before building took place.

The village stands 406 feet above sea level.

Turn right, up the avenue of beech trees. On your right is Drumrossie Woods, and on your left the new housing estate, Mayfield, named after the home of the builder, Mr. Gordon Souter.

The land from Beechcroft Terrace to the Aberdeen road was once Beech Croft farmed by John Russell & Son. They had three cows and two horses which they required in the running of their merchant business.

High Street

A little further and you come to the Shevock (from the Gaelic, placid little burn). This burn was one of the old village boundaries. Cross by the Bridge of Insch sometimes called M'Cracken's Briggie, after Doctor M'Cracken, who built his house and surgery (the one on your left) in the 1860s. Behind the house he had a barn and a stable for his horse.

Mrs. M'Cracken (front right) with her guests.
Back row from the left: *Mr. Willie Beattie, tea planter from Ceylon, her sister Miss Jessie Beattie, Dunnydeer Farm, Miss McWilliam, whose brother Mr. John McWilliam was headmaster of the Parochial School in Commerce Street from 1875-95. She kept house for him in the School House in High Street.*
Front left: *Miss Aggie Forsyth, daughter of the baker and church organist who later married an Indian doctor and went to live in Ceylon (Sri Lanka). (Mrs M'Cracken was a ten month old baby when Queen Victoria came to the throne in 1837).*
By J. Laing & Co. Photographers, Insch.
Given to me by Miss Bella Horne.

The house to your right was once the Congregational Church Manse.

Further to the right are the Tennis Courts, in a pleasant and sheltered situation, one of the best in the north-east. They were opened in 1922, provided and maintained by a committee of local people. Players have competed successfully in north-east leagues competitions but in the recent past a dwindling membership has prevented them taking part.

Near the courts is the site of the old curling pond. Insch and Upper Garioch Curling Club was in being from 1889 until 1954.

Carry on up High Street but pause to look at Woodburn, built of red granite. In 1874 Colonel Alexander Sebastian Leith Hay C.B. of Rannes and Leith Hall granted the feu, or piece of land, on which Woodburn stands to George Benzie who had inherited the property and was a miner, residing at Sandycreek in the Colony of Victoria, Australia. A dwelling house had already been erected on the feu, surrounded by stone and lime walls at least four feet high and a dwarf wall with iron railings. George Benzie was not allowed to erect buildings without approval from his landlord and "shall have no byre, stable or other outhouse opening into or fronting the Public Road". He was not entitled "to deposit or set down any dunghills or other nuisances or obstructions in front of the said premises". He also had to take his share of maintenance of main drains and cesspools and provide a flagstone path at least three feet in breadth in front of his house.

George Benzie did not return to Scotland. Woodburn was sold and by the 1880s Miss Helen Abel was running her dressmaking business, here, employing several girls. It was their custom, when finishing a wedding dress for each girl to pull a hair from her head and stitch it into the hem as a good luck token.

Next door is a modern bungalow. On this site, stood the United Free Church Manse.

Across the street is the modern Fire Station, opened in 1963. It all began in 1892 when the Dean of Guild proposed to the Council that a Firemaster be appointed and six or eight young men be trained to handle the hose and prepare themselves to act in the event of fire. In 1948 the government took over the running of the local council fire brigades. Mr Peter Webster, Senior, became leading fireman in charge of the Retained Brigade. Mr. Frank Anderson, Senior, followed as sub-officer in 1958 and in 1972 Mr. Sandy Davidson became sub-officer. Shields and cups frequently pass through Insch Fire Station. In 1981 they won two shields, one being the Arbuthnott, for the best retained fire station in the region, and three cups, one for the champion driver, won by Mr. Bob Simpson.

There were two voluntary fire brigades during the 1939 - 45 war.

It was on this place, where the fire station now stands, that the people of Insch built their United Free Church. In the olden times the heritors (land owners) were responsible for providing a church and choosing a minister. At the time of the Disruption in 1843 many people in Scotland broke away from the established or parish church wishing to be "free" to have their own church and choose their own minister. The members of Insch United Free Church also provided a United Free Church School for their children. Long afterwards, in the 1940s when the congregations were re-united the building was no longer used as a church and became an egg-grading station.

Walk along to the entrance to Alexander Street. (In 1892, when the streets were named and the houses numbered, the name of the superior of Insch was Colonel Alexander Sebastian Leith Hay.) From here you will see the present school. The original building, opened in 1899, has been extended several times. On 17th November, 1899 John Galloway inspected the school and these are his remarks entered and signed in the School Log Book. "Present were 119 boys and 114 girls. The new buildings are delightful for work and to the eye."

Once Insch Higher Grade Public School it is now a primary school.

Turn again to look at High Street. The house next to the Kirk Yard is known as The Old School House. From the 1842 Statistical Account, "a few years ago a detached dwelling house was built for the school master". This building altered and enlarged over the years remained the school house of Insch until the early 1950s. Headmasters of the Parochial School in Commerce Street (now Simpson's Garage) and of the school in Alexander Street lived here.

Now, you have come to the most historic place in Insch. Open the iron gate and go in. Saint Drostan, who was a relative of Saint Columba, is said to have brought Christianity to this part of Scotland. He was the Patron Saint of the old Kirk of Insch. We do not know when the first St. Drostan's was built but there is a record of a church in Insch from the twelfth century. At that time the lands of Insch belonged to David, Earl of Huntington and of the Garioch, whose people had come to Britain with the Normans and whose brother was King William the Lion of Scotland. As a thank offering for his safe return from a crusade he founded Lindores Abbey in Fife and gave his land in the Garioch for its upkeep. In return the Abbey had to provide a church for the people of Insch.

When Earl David acquired his lands the valleys of The Shevock and Gadie were already rich fertile ground. Teinds to the Abbey were paid in corn and flour rather than the more common teinds of butter and cheese from the pastoral lands.

Part of the ruins of Lindores Abbey near Newburgh, Fife.
Photographed in 1986.

Before and after the Reformation in the church, which took place in the middle of the sixteenth century, ownership of the lands of Garioch passed to various lairds but in many instances feu duties continued to be paid to Lindores. The farm of Edderlick in Premnay paid their last feu duty in 1967.

Fortunately, there are some photographs of the church, the gable end of which you can see. The belfry dated 1613 has the initials of the minister, M.J.L. (Minister John Logie). The bell, which was removed to a new church, was made by Albert Gely in 1706.

Two Aberdeen Silver Communion Cups were presented to the church in 1697 by John Rose, a landowner. They are now used in the Communion Services held in the church in Western Road.

There is a record of church services being interrupted in the seventeenth century by Highlanders who had come down to raid the livestock in the

St. Drostan's Kirk in High Street.   Given to me by Miss J. Russell.

4

Garioch. There was no collection at Insch Kirk on 28th April 1689, the kirk being dissolved in the middle of a sermon.

In 1882 the old church was condemned as unsafe and pulled down. Not many people remember anything about the worshippers in that church. Miss Bella Horne tells me this story of her grandfather, George Forsyth who was born in 1826. He was a master baker and had his shop where the baker shop is today. Every Saturday he put bricks in his oven and on Sunday morning carried them down the street and placed them in the family pew. How grateful his family must have been. We read that, in 1842, the building, the walls of which were four feet thick, was without plaster or ceiling.

After The Disruption, the congregation noticed that their minister, when in his pulpit, took care to avert his eyes from the new Free Church across the street.

There are many interesting stones in the kirk yard. The long coffin slab by the gable wall is one of the oldest lettered stones in Scotland. The inscription in Latin (Pray for the soul of Randolph the Priest) was preserved because the stone had been buried for a long time and was uncovered in the early nineteenth century when alterations were being made to the church. The priest was the Bishop of Aberdeen and it is said he was in the habit of walking around his diocese, became ill and died while staying in his residence on Dunnydeer (the hill to the west with the ruined castle).

There is a memorial ˌstone to Walter Roger, who on a Sunday in February 1746 disarmed David Tyrie, a Jacobite, who was threatening the min-ister with a pistol as he read a government proclamation in favour of the Hanoverian King George II. This tall grey granite stone was erected by Alexander Roger, a descendant of Walter, the "Muckle Whig" and is to the memory of many Rogers from 1589.

If you have time to look around, there are many more.

Before you leave look at the north wall. There are two or three old buildings built into it. In 1684 the minister "Gave of his own glebe a place for the parish to build a school-house in upon the church yard dyke and north side" (Rev. R.S. Kemp B.D.). (School-house meaning school.) It is still there today, the first recorded school in Insch, with door and window facing High Street. There was an inner door leading through to the adjoining cottage.

Look, once more, over to The Old School House and grounds. In the thirteenth century an acre was allocated for a manse next to the church so it is very likely that the early manse of Insch stood here. From the Statistical Account of 1842 "The present manse, which is about half a mile distant from the church, the old site in the village having been relinquished, was built in 1771".

At the gate, turn to your right and walk along the pavement until you come to the Free Masons Lodge. This building was the Congregational Church of Insch. Built in 1866, it was a place of worship until the beginning of World War II. Opposite is J. & A. Forsyth's shop. In 1815 Alexander Wilson, a master carpenter, had left his birth place, Old Town, Rothney, bought and occupied the premises which stood where the shop is now. He was one of the first people in the area to join the Congregational Church in Huntly, walking there every

Sunday along the old road past Christ Kirk. For forty-five years he taught in various Sunday Schools and in 1812 was the founder and father of Sabbath-schools in Insch. During the time he lived in this house he became very ill with typhus fever, an infectious disease which occurred from time to time in the village. Some years after moving to Insch he purchased the property opposite. So often did he give the use of the upper floor free of charge to anyone lecturing on moral or scientific subjects, that it became known as "The Insch Hall". He is the only Insch person, that I know of, who had his biography written and published — "The Life of Alexander Wilson" 1780 - 1858 by the Reverend Thomas Brisbane.

Mr. and Mrs. Wilson had a daughter Jane who married John Russell. Together they founded the business known as John Russell & Son. The business grew and the buildings grew until they looked very much like they are today. During the one hundred years the Russell family were merchants in Insch, they employed tailors, milliners, dress-makers, shop-assistants and a man to feed and look after their cows and horses. Each department had someone in charge, tailor/cutter, head milliner, shop foreman, involving in all about thirty-five to forty people. After World War I it was not an uncommon sight to see a tailor on one leg and a crutch go off to work at Russell's or any of the other tailoring establishments in the village.

The downstairs room on the left became known as "The Tweed Room' the speciality of Mr. John Russell's son George. He travelled over Scotland, frequently to Shetland, selecting the finest tweeds and knitwear. His Tweed Room gained a wide reputation and was patronised by the local people, visitors in the season and some members of the Royal Family, including two queens. Coming along here in the 1950s it is just possible that you would have found a small crowd waiting for the Queen Mother and Princess Margaret to emerge from Russell's.

Walk past Forsyth's shop and the adjoining house. On the gable end are rings which were used for tethering horses while they were being shod. It is most likely that the smiddy which stood here belonged, at one time, to Provost William Martin. His dwelling house was just across the yard, facing on to Martin Road. It was the custom, when shoeing a filly for the first time, for the owner and the blacksmith to have a dram together. Callander's shop was — conveniently — just across the street. The last person to carry out his business here was not a blacksmith but a coach builder Mr. Alexander Middleton more often known as Chap Chap. He had previously worked for a firm of coach builders in the old school buildings (now Simpson's Garage) in Commerce Street. The coaches were the horse-drawn kind and he fitted out the interiors. That business inevitably drew to a close and it was here in his later years that Chap Chap worked, turning his skill to quality workmanship on household furniture. In his younger days Alexander Middleton was a keen athlete, competing and winning medals in local games, such as the Odd Fellows Picnic.

From 1824 - 1913 at Jericho, just a few miles from Insch, there was a distillery and in a shop across the High Street owned by William Callander you would have been invited to buy "Benachie Pure Highland Malt" — a two gallon Pig or a bottle bearing the slogan "there's nae sair heids in Benachie".

Later the Insch Hand Laundry Company occupied this shop. Next door there was a sweet, ale (lemonade) and pie shop.

In earlier times the business premises of James Bisset and his son George stood on this part of High Street. They sold drapery, boots and shoes, paper hangings, carpets, ironmongery, china, groceries, seeds and much more. Mr. James Bisset had formerly carried on his business in the busy post town of Old Rayne which was situated on the coach route to the north. On learning that the railway was to pass through Insch he foresaw the growth of trade here. When one of his apprentices, John Russell (who later became the founder of the firm John Russell & Son) heard the

news, he wept with frustration at the thought of moving to such a backwater as Insch. In 1861 the population of Insch was 411.

George's brother John was a bank agent and Provost of Insch at the end of the nineteenth century. He and his family lived at Thornhill at the top of Charles Street and employed a family governess.

It was here, too, in High Street that the society of Good Templars held their weekly meeting.

Look over to the Clydesdale Bank. It was on this site that Alexander Roger, Baron Bailie, bank agent, merchant and postmaster opened the first post office in Insch in 1857. By the mid-1850s mail was carried to Insch by rail. Previously Old Rayne had been the nearest post

Bisset's Buildings. The upper part of the other two storey building to the right of the photograph was known as The Insch Hall. Entry was by an outside stair at the back. Loaned by Dr. C. Bernard.

town. Letters were delivered there by the mail coach on its way from Aberdeen to Huntly. A letter carrier then brought them the last 3½ miles to Insch at 1d. a letter.

After the bank was built Alexander Roger moved his post office to where the chip shop is today, beside the bus stop. The frontage of his first shop is still here in Insch. If you care to retrace your footsteps to J. & A. Forsyth's you will see it on the part of the shop next to the corner. The position of the posting box is quite clearly marked.

Loaned by Mrs. H. Gordon, Tayloch.

In 1878 Alexander Roger's son, also Alexander Roger, J.P. and Baron Bailie of Insch Town Council left a legacy to the people of Insch District that the residue of his estate be invested and the revenue used "for the purpose of providing nursing, medical and other comforts" for those who were in need. The Alexander Roger Sick Fund is still being distributed every Christmas.

As well as helping individuals the fund contributed from 1910 to the District Nursing Association and from 1925 to Insch and District War Memorial Hospital, providing for a stay in hospital or an operation for those who could not afford to pay.

In 1893 Mrs. Panton gifted a silver Communion Cup, after the style of the John Rose cups, to Insch Established Church in memory of her uncle and cousin, Alexander Roger, Senior and Alexander Roger, Junior.

Loaned by Mrs. H. Gordon, Tayloch.

"Tailor" Smith lived in one of the houses in High Street. He and his friend "Baker" Forsyth played draughts every Saturday evening until one momentous Saturday when they did not finish the game. On Sunday, during the church service, the baker worked out his next move, this way and that. On Monday he went to his friend and said to him that there was to be no more draughts "when

Village decorated in honour of the opening of the Waterworks.   Dr. Currie's Book.

it comes between me and my Maker" and there never was.

The Square

SUNDAY observance was a solemn thing. Dr. Currie writes of what he found in the mid-nineteenth century church records, "these were times when it was forbidden for one to walk in the fields, meadows or streets, to sit at ones' door or in ones' garden".

Dr. Currie lived where Cooper & Harper's shop is today. He left us a

Procession through village on opening of Waterworks. Dr. G. Currie on horseback.   Dr. Currie's Book.

Red Cross Hospital, Drumrossie House, 1914 - 18.
Loaned by Miss M. Mitchell.

wonderful legacy in the form of a book entitled "The Annals of Insch" which he began writing on 1st January, 1889. It contains historical notes, observations on people and events of the time and newspaper cuttings. He writes of his concern over the prevalence of epidemic disorders and the quality of the water from the village pumps. In his book there is a photograph taken on what must have been a triumphant day for him. The streets were decorated with flowers, evergreens and bunting. There was a fine procession waiting to leave, horses and carriages, people on foot, Dr. G.B. Currie on horseback. A strict order of precedence was observed, as in all processions, and was reported in great detail in the press, naming the owner of the carriage and the persons aboard. The occasion was the opening of the Insch and Rothney Water Works on 4th September, 1890.

During their 80 years the firm of Cooper & Harper has sold groceries. In earlier times they had a drapery department with tailoring, sold antiques and ran three vans, two grocery and one drapery.

You are now in The Square. We do not know where the village of Insch began. Some historians think that a small village would have grown round the church. There is a record of Robert the Bruce, after the Battle of Bannockburn, granting feus (pieces of land) with grazing rights to ten to twelve of his faithful followers from this area. The late Provost John Anderson in a letter dated 1943 states that he was shown the title deeds of one of these feus which is in Latin on sheepskin.

Cross The Square, to the right is Drumrossie Street. Just over the bridge is the gate to the avenue leading to Drumrossie House. The main part of the present house dates from the eighteenth

Drumrossie Lodge, Insch.
Loaned by Mrs. H. Gordon, Tayloch.

century but Drumrossie history goes back to thirteenth century and Lindores. It lies outside the old Burgh of Insch across the burn in Rothney of which it was the manor place. In the past, local agricultural shows and picnics were held in the grounds. In World War I Drumrossie House was a Red Cross Hospital. If you walk out Drumrossie Street and along Denwell Road you will find that you are facing almost due north.

On the corner where Market Street and Drumrossie Street meet there stood a tall house known as The Neuk (see cover of book). In 1693 William Logie, merchant and burgess of the burgh (which meant he had been appointed a freeman by the bailies) along with his wife, requested a feu from the landowner, Mr. Alexander Rose. They wished to build on this corner site, between two merchants' houses, a house with a garden. A symbolic handing over of

earth and stone took place at the Mill of Insch, performed by the miller who was a bailie of the burgh and represented the landowner. Mr. & Mrs. Logie were granted the right to dig turf in the peat-moss of Melschach and on the Hill of Foudland. They also had the right to quarry hard and free stone for the purpose of repairing buildings and erecting boundary walls. There were several witnesses to this event, including the school master, Mr. William Leslie whose name appears in the 1696 Poll Book. The 1693 title to Mr. & Mrs. Logie's property is written on parchment, smooth and silky to the touch, coloured light brown. It crackles slightly when opened. Inside, the colour of the parchment is paler and the fine hand-writing in Latin is clear.

In 1836 this building became the property of Mr. John Courage, a watchmaker. His shop adjoined the house and faced on to Market Street. He gifted the D.J. Riddel of Aberdeen clock which is in the Parish Church in Western Road. Other Insch clockmakers were Charles Sim and George Dallas.

The cottages adjoining The Neuk in Drumrossie street were latterly owned by Mr. George Russell. He let them at a nominal rent to elderly people along with some of his other properties in the village.

All the buildings which stood where Dunchavin Cottages are now, were pulled down in 1961. The high wall of The Neuk came down on Hogmanay Day.

Pause and listen before you proceed down Market Street. Here comes the Town Crier, resplendent in his uniform, clanging his bell about to make an announcement. Until the beginning of the twentieth century the Town Council employed a Town Crier and supplied him with a uniform and a bell. All that remains now is the bell.

Market Street

BEFORE the present houses were built, the left-hand side of Market Street looked very different. To the back of S. & J. Davidson's shop there was an arched entrance to a courtyard around which houses were built. There was also a house built over the archway. There was no other entrance to the square. All that is left now is a high wall running parallel to Commerce Street. It is still visible from the far end of the street looking back towards The Square. A little further along and on the same side was a house which stood well forward with a rounded gable. I have been told that it was possible to sit in the window and knit and at the same time view all that was taking place in High Street.

Pass Dunchavin Cottages. On the right is the Market Mere, the market place of olden times. Here, by the end of the eighteenth century you could have bought a pair of brogues for which Insch was well known. By 1849 there were eight cattle markets being held annually. As late as the beginning of this century travelling folk were pitching their tents here and gipsies were coming with their horse-drawn caravans.

Behind Market Square and down by the burn was a street called Dubbystile and a row of wooden houses known as Timmer Terrace leading to the Gas Works which stood where the Council sheds are today.

By the 1830s the Gas Works, which was run by a company, was in production. From the 1842 Statistical Account we learn that "most of the shops and dwelling houses have been for some years lighted with gas". Before the coming of the railway, English coal was brought from Aberdeen to Inverurie by canal and 14 miles by horse and cart to Insch.

For many years Mr. Billy Dressel was gas man. He is remembered by people who lived in Insch between the Wars. As well as being responsible for producing gas at the required pressure, day and night, he cleaned and maintained the street lamps, both gas and paraffin. In the morning he would set off at a run, his ladder on his shoulder, prop the ladder against a lamp, climb up, clean the glass, check the mantel and if paraffin was needed fill the lamp, down and on to the next one until all the lamps in the village had been attended to. Approximately 5.00 pm would find him shouldering his ladder again, this time to light the lamps and about 10.30 pm he would be off again to extinguish the lights. There was no street lighting in the mornings and none at all in the summer. At times the Town Council economised by lighting fewer lamps when the moon was full.

For Mr. Dressel, his work with the Gas Company was just a side line. He was the Insch plumber and he also found time to be a member of the church choir. The Gas Works closed down in the mid-1930s with the arrival of electricity to the village.

Walk on to Golf Terrace. What is now the children's play area was once the Market Stance and the Commonty Lands. Villagers used to graze their cattle here during the day, walking them home in the evening. There are still some buildings, in the village, which were at one time used as byres. By the 1950s only two or three people were keeping cows.

It was on the Market Stance that the first cricket match was played in Insch against Huntly on 26th July, 1866. Later, cricket was played in a field in front of the hospital.

Beyond the play area is the nine-hole Golf Course re-opened in 1982 largely through five years voluntary effort. Insch lost its old course to the Army in World War II. Mr. James Grant, former champion of the old Club, was given the honour of being the first to tee-off at the opening of the new. But the Insch Golf Club's badge bears the

Established Church Choir Picnic — 1920s
Front Row: *Billy Dressel, Jimmy Brewster, Jamie Grassick.*
Middle Row: *??, Willie Moir, Maggie Scott, Ella Stewart, Annabel Merchant, Bella Philip (who lives in High Street), Cissie Stewart (Church Organist), Rev. John Mack.*
Back Row: *Willie Park, Winnie Stewart, Mary Grassick, Lizzie Wilson, John Fraser.*
Given to me by Miss B. Horne.

figure three. The earliest course was round the foot of the Hill of Dunnydeer.

Pause on the very old bridge which crosses the Valentine Burn. In his "Annals of Insch" Dr. Currie says that the castle or tower on Dunnydeer was consecrated to St. Valentine. Others say that Valentine is from the Gaelic meaning burn of the town of wealth in cattle. On the right-hand side of the bridge, somewhere near the side of the burn was the Mottoch or Mottie Well (well with medicinal virtues), the water from which was said to make the best grog.

Miss Bella Horne tells me that in the summer her grandmother Mrs. Forsyth, along with other Insch house-wives, would rise at 4.30 am on a Monday and take their washing to the burn. When all was clean she would then spread the garments on the bleaching green, an area of the Commonty specially reserved the purpose.

Across the burn is the football pitch and the playing field. The belt of trees to the north and west was planted by the Insch and Rothney Town Council to commemorate the Coronation of Queen Elizabeth, 1953. Each member of the council then planted a popular tree in the foreground.

Insch Football Club is at least 80 years old. In the beginning there were two teams, The Rose and The Thistle playing in the Upper Donside League. After World War II they became Insch Amateur Football Club and in 1976 they entered Aberdeen Amateur Association. There are many old newspaper photo-graphs of the Club receiving cups and trophies. Two of their players who have gone on to play at higher grades are Derek Reid and Derek Stephen.

Across the road to the right is the remains of the old sheep dipper. Further to the right over on Denwell Road is Bassie Cottage. One of the buildings was for a time used as a slaughter house. The land north of the burn extending from the trees to Denwell Road was the old Bass Croft.

"In 1686 is the following, which is the first recorded notice of the Bass, a small piece of land which for a century and a half belonged to and was managed by the Kirk Session, till handed over to the Parochial Board, and which saves the poor rates to the extent of nearly £14 yearly". "It may be observed in the passing that the Bass was purchased with money used for the 'publick good' quite a separate fund from the 'poors monie', and not given to the poor at all". (Historical Notes on the Parish of Insch to the end of the seventeenth century by Rev. Robert S. Kemp.)

The Parochial Board appointed an Inspector of the Poor and a Poor's House was built on the corner where Market Street and Golf Terrace now meet.

Mr Alexander Roger, in his time, expressed a wish to see a hospital built on the Bass.

Commerce Street

TURN back to The Square. If you had come to Insch on a feeing market day you would have found the Square and part of Commerce Street crowded with farmers and farm servants, male and female, bargaining their wages for the next six months. This was a twice yearly event in May and November. On such occasions the baker made a special treat for the bairns — gingerbread men and horses. And the baker shop was just where it is today.

Carry on up Commerce Street. The first street on the left is Martin Road named after Mr. William Martin, blacksmith and provost. He was provost from 1858 to 1887 and lived in what is now the block of three terraced houses, but in his time was a one storied thatched cottage. The small buildings next to the car park must be some of the oldest in Insch and were the barn and byre where he kept his cow. His name is the first on the provost's chain but William Martin was by no means the first provost of Insch. (He was elected in 1778.) Provost Martin was a kindly hearted man who sometimes liked to "mak a night oot" at the Commercial Hotel with his greatest friend Mr. John Gartly. One pitch black night when leaving the hotel they took the wrong turning. On not finding the usual landmarks John Gartley said, "Dod Provie, I canna see my pump", to which he replied, "an I doot I've tint my closie".

Two years before Provost Martin retired, "his friends at Insch" presented him with a gold locket and chain. Recently I was shown this beautiful locket and chain by his great-grand

Provost Martin.
From Dr. Currie's book.

niece. He is wearing it in this photograph from Dr. Currie's "Annals of Insch".

If you had come walking down Martin Road about 100 years ago you could possibly have found your way barred by a horse. John Russell & Son had a threshing mill housed in the part

Given to me by Miss J. Russell.

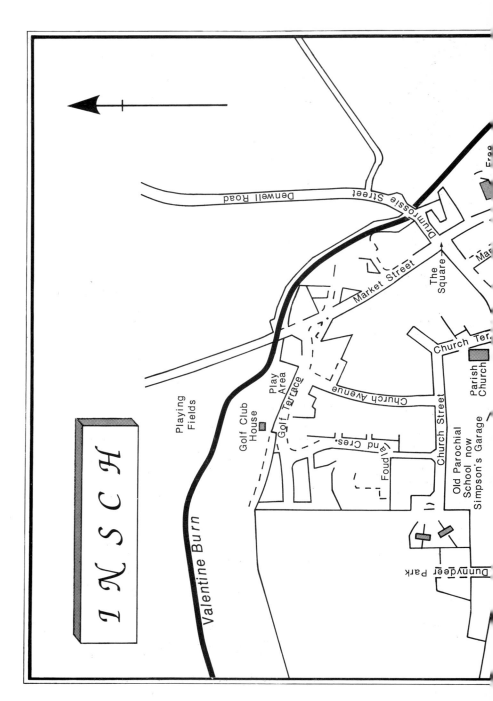

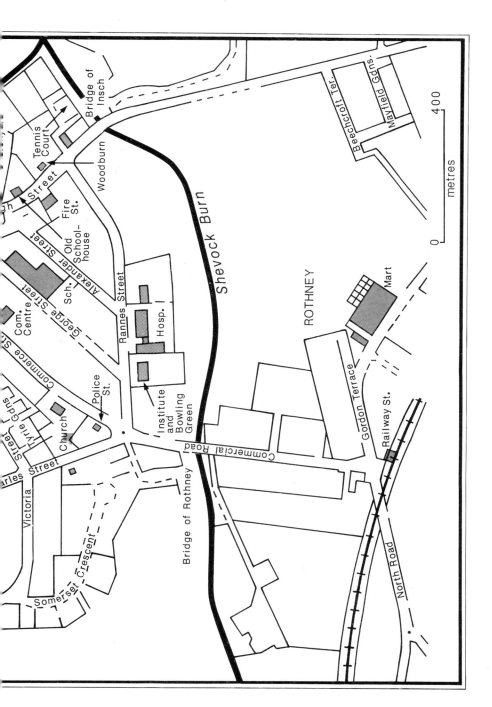

Bridge of Insch

Tennis Court

Woodburn

Street

Fire St.

Old School-house

Alexander Street

George Street

Sch.

Rannes Street

Com. Centre

Commerce St.

Police St.

Church

Tyrie Gdns.

Supd.

...les Street

Victoria Street

Somerset Crescent

Institute and Bowling Green

Hosp.

Shevock Burn

ROTHNEY

Bridge of Rothney

Commercial Road

Mart

Gordon Terrace

Railway St.

Beechcroft Ter.

Mayfield Gdns.

North Road

0   400
metres

17

of their premises which bordered Martin Road. The horse, which was harnessed to a shaft, walked in a continuous circle producing the one horse-power required to drive the mill.

The next name on the provost's chain is John Gartly. He lived at 16 Commerce Street, just opposite Martin Road, and was for many years Inspector of the Poor. He was one of the original promoters of the Insch Public Hall and afterwards a director.

Walk until you come to the fork in the road. Alvah Cottage, the house in the triangle, was at one time the Insch "jile".

Turn your back on Alvah Cottage and look at this photograph from the 1930s. (Page 15)

The double cottage in the background was called Grove Cottage. To the right was a watchmaker and jeweller. Watches could be bought or cleaned, oiled and repaired. Next door was a boot and shoe shop where the shoemaker spent a great deal of his time fitting new soles and heels to his customers' partly-worn footwear. Just out of sight, next door to the bakers were two saddlers shops. Saddlers made all harnesses required for farm horses, the saddle, the collar and all the smaller items. Leather was brought north from England. He sold ribbons and raffia to decorate horses for shows. At harvest time he was kept very busy repairing binder cloths (long strips of canvas used in the reaping machine). Mr. John Milne was the last master saddler in Insch. Some of his work is exhibited in the National Museum of Antiquities in Edinburgh.

On the right is Mr. Farquhar's chemist shop. In the centre of the picture marching down the street, is the Insch and Rothney Pipe Band.

The band was formed in 1927. Its first Drum-Major was Mr. Mike Mac-Donald whom you see in this photograph. He was followed by Drum-Major Mr. James Cran. In 1955 the Press and Journal published pictures of the band. At that time Mr. Alan Henderson, who

Celebrations on the Coronation of King Edward VII 22nd June, 1911.   Given to me by Miss B. Horne.

The King of Spain travelling by car from Fyvie Castle to Leith Hall. Mr Leith-Hay is seated by the driver. (The King would no doubt, have included a visit to a Spanish gentleman who had married a Scot and lived in the mansion house of Wardhouse — now a ruin.)
Given to me by Miss B. Horne.

had been a drummer with the Gordon Highlanders, was Drum-Major. Mr. George Angus, who had been a piper with the Gordons was Pipe-Major. Mr. Peter Webster, who was later to become Drum-Major was bass drummer. There were three brothers and one sister of the McCombie family. The band always turned out to lead the procession on a special occasion in Insch, be it royal celebration or children's picnic. At weekends they were often invited to play in neighbouring towns. Everyone who told me of their memories of the band showed great pride in its quality.

Look up now to the tallest building in Insch, the Parish church of Insch, Leslie, Premnay and Oyne, a place of many memories. Built in 1883 by the heritors and named the Established Church it stood in its glory on the edge of the village. During World War II the United Free Church or East Church shared a minister with the Established Church and in 1944 East and West Congregations were united. In 1983 when an exhibition of mementos of 100 years of the churches was being prepared several people told me of an abiding memory they had of German prisoners of war singing Silent Night at a war time Christmas Service.

Fresh in my memory is the beauty of the Christmas Service 1984 with our Insch congregation united with Leslie, Premnay and Oyne.

If you would like to learn more about the churches in Insch read Dr. Douglas Stewart's book "Insch Parish Church 1883 - 1983".

Look up once again to the clock tower. Its building was financed by the village folk and for one hundred years maintained by them.

Behind and to the right and left of the church is Church Street, Terrace and Avenue, Russell Street, Valentine Street, Foudland Crescent, all Council property, the building of which began in the 1930s.

19

Personal photographs and local views on postcards were very popular in Victorian and Edwardian times. Once a week Robert Brown, who was a photographer in Inverurie, hired a small studio which was situated to the right of the church.

You will find on many of the old postcards of Insch the name Farquhar, Chemist or Wilson, Chemist.

Almost opposite the church in Western Road is the Church Hall with the date 1901 over the door. To help raise funds for the building of the hall the Reverend R. Kemp B.D. had published a booklet entitled "Historical Notes on the Parish of Insch to the end of the seventeenth century". He was, incidentally, the minister who preached his first sermon with a black eye which he had sustained on the Insch cricket field the previous day.

Beyond the church hall and to the left is the housing estate Tyrie Gardens, named in 1968 by the Tyrees from America whose ancestors the Tyries of Dunnydeer lived in a manor house on the banks of the Shevock. All that is left of the house now is a fragment of wall by a group of trees which can be seen from the Kennethmont road.

Red hawthorn trees were planted in the gardens by the Tyrees to mark the opening ceremony.

Mr. Alex. J.M. Troup, a journalist, lived at Ythan Grove, Victoria Street. He had a book published by the Aberdeen Journal Office in 1893 — "Fontythan and Other Poems". He was known locally as the "wheeper-in" (a school attendance officer).

Retrace your steps back to Alvah Cottage. If you had come here in the last century, during school playtime you would have found the corner full of children, some well dressed wearing boots and some "barfit". There were two schools in this part of the village. The

Insch school children at play. The Free Church School and Grove Cottage in the background.
Loaned by Mr. & Mrs. P. Russell.

building which is now owned by Messrs. Simpson, Agricultural Engineers was the Parochial School provided by the heritors. The old classroom windows can be seen on the west wall.

From the 1842 Statistical Account we learn that "the present Parochial school-house possesses ample and superior accommodation having been built a few years ago". (School-house meaning school.)

The other school was the Free Church School and it stood roughly where the Television shop is today. In the 1840s the congregation of the Free Church provided a school and appointed a school master for the education of their children. Children of the Established Church would have continued to attend the Parochial School.

The Education Act of 1872 made school attendance compulsory. No longer were the heritors and the churches responsible for education. School boards were formed on a parish basis. In 1877 Insch School became overcrowded and twenty pupils from Rothney were expelled. Rothney was in the parish of Premnay and the school board expected the pupils to walk to Premnay school. But a classroom was found for them in Western Road.

Perhaps the United Free Church school came into use again. By 1880 they were re-admitted to Insch School. The Public Hall was used as temporary classrooms and the school was extended. When the present owners bought the premises they saw evidence of alterations to the original school rooms and just to prove that our Insch centenarian, Doctor George Cooper, had been a pupil, his coat peg was still on the wall. (Dr. Cooper died in July 1985, aged 102.)

By 1898 plans for a new school had been approved and one year later the school in Alexander Street was opened. In that same year the headmaster often wrote in the School Log Book of his disappointment at his pupils poor attendance at school. At busy times some children were kept at home to assist their parents, but absence was due, too, to illness, frequently of an infectious kind, among pupils and members of staff. On 14th March there is this sad entry in the Log Book, "Another case today of scarlet fever. This time it has occurred as before in the infant room. Diphtheria still raging and another death reported." On a happier note — the children were always given a holiday for St. Sair's Market in early July.

Opposite the old school in Commerce Street is Insch Community Centre. In 1869 the foundation stone of this building was laid by Alexander Roger, Senior, Baron Bailie and one of the oldest inhabitants of Insch. It was named

DAVID O. SELZNICK's production of MARGARET MITCHELL's
GONE WITH THE WIND
in TECHNICOLOR starring
CLARK VIVIEN LESLIE OLIVIA
GABLE · LEIGH · HOWARD · DeHAVILLAND
A Metro-Goldwyn-Mayer Re-presentation

GLEN CINEMAS
INSCH

The management have pleasure in presenting this famous film which has broken all records wherever it has been shown.

On its first release in London it ran for four-and-a-half years before all the people who wanted to see it had done so, and they still want to go back to see it again.

Now we consider ourselves fortunate in being able to show it to you.

To see this film is a MUST for those who have not already seen it, and a very welcome repeat for those who have.

Book your seats early for the greatest film since the talkies came.

THE MANAGER

Loaned by Miss Thelma Smith.

PROGRAMME FOR THE MONTH OF DECEMBER, 1950

Saturday, 2nd December—
LEO GORCEY, HUNTZ HALL in
GHOSTS IN THE NIGHT
Co-Starring BELA LUGOSI and AVA GARDNER
Also TRAILING DOUBLE TROUBLE

Wednesday, 6th December—
RITA HAYWORTH, WILLIAM HOLDEN in
THE LOVES OF CARMEN
(Technicolor)
Also TRAPPED BY A BLONDE and CLOSE UP

Saturday, 9th December—
BETTY GRABLE, JOHN PAYNE in
the Lavish Technicolor
SPRINGTIME IN THE ROCKIES
with CARMEN MIRANDA and CESAR ROMERO

Wednesday, 13th December—
MADELEINE CARROLL, FRED MacMURRAY in
DON'T TRUST YOUR HUSBAND
Also THE CONNOR'S CASE

Saturday, 16th December—
VICTOR MATURE, BRIAN DONLEVY in
THE KISS OF DEATH
with COLEEN GRAY and RICHARD WIDMARK

Wednesday, 20th December—
SONJA HENIE, JOHN PAYNE, JACK OAKIE in
KATINA

Saturday, 23rd December—
SABU, GAIL RUSSELL, TURHAN BEY in
SONG OF INDIA
Also Charles Starrett, Smiley Burnette in
STRANGE DISAPPEARANCE

Wednesday, 27th December—
TO BE ANNOUNCED

Saturday, 30th December—
BETTY GRABLE, VICTOR MATURE in
SONG OF THE ISLANDS
with JACK OAKIE and THOMAS MITCHELL

ANDREW PETRIE
Building Contractor
2 MARKET STREET, INSCH
Telephone: INSCH 82
All Kinds of Building Repairs, Modernising of
Dwellings, Byres and Farm Steadings, Specialising in
Tiled Fireplaces, Hearths and Kerbs, etc.
WORKMANSHIP GUARANTEED
All Orders Receive Personal Attention

COMMERCIAL HOTEL
INSCH, ABERDEENSHIRE
Under New Management
7 DAYS' LICENCE
BREAKFASTS, MORNING COFFEE, LUNCH,
AFTERNOON TEAS and HIGH TEAS
Hot and Cold in All Bedrooms
WEDDINGS, and SOCIAL EVENTS, BUS DRIVES
and PRIVATE PARTIES Fully Catered For
Telephone: INSCH 9

GORDON TERRACE CAFE
INSCH
On the Aberdeen Main Road
MORNING COFFEES, LUNCHEONS,
AFTERNOON TEAS, HIGH TEAS, SNACKS,
MINERALS, ICES FRUIT & CONFECTIONERY
Picnic Parties Catered For

Loaned by Miss Thelma Smith.

Insch Public Hall and was run by a limited company. Two bottles containing coins, newspapers, etc., were buried at a corner of the hall.

There was a flat upstairs for the hall keeper.

Many uses have been made of this building. In the nineteenth century The Volunteers drilled here and between the wars it was where the V.A.Ds. received their instructions. It has been used as a temporary school and a temporary church. After the old church in High Street had been condemned in 1882 and before the church in Western Road had been completed, services were held in the small hall of the Public Hall. Mr. George Forsyth, the baker, who then lived at Grove Cottage, had handles fitted to his harmonium. Each week-end it was carried to and from the hall.

Many concerts have been held here. On the evening of the 17th March, 1949 Insch Strathspey and Reel Society held a Scottish Concert. The conductor was Mr. W. Cruickshank, the station master. There were visiting soloists and Mr. John Y. Murray played his own compositions on the fiddle, "Drumrossie Woods", "Dunnydeer", "The Shevock Burn" and "Mist o'er Bennachie". He had the chemist shop that was formerly Mr. Farquhar's. Mr. Murray played by ear and whistled his tunes to Mrs. Cameron who recorded them on paper for him. Mrs. L.M. Cameron L.R.A.M. accompanied the soloists in this concert.

When a film was shown, the Public Hall became The Glen Cinema.

Dances and balls have been held here, too. On the evening of a dinner-dance the doors and windows of the hall were curtained in chintz and the seats covered in matching material. Long tables were laid with white cloths and dinner was brought in from one of the hotels. There was a temporary, cold, draughty and romantic corridor built between the hall and the armoury (from the days of the Volunteers), where drinks were sold. On such occasions Insch Public Hall seemed as grand as a castle ballroom.

The Public Hall was the home of the Town Council. There are records of feuers meetings and burghers meetings from 1819 but it was not until the 1880s that the title town council appeared. At first councillors were elected by the householders of the burgh but latterly by all, within the burgh, whose name appeared on the voters roll. They liaised with the Superior of the town, the laird of Leith Hall estates, regarding the maintenance of the streets and pavements, the management of the Commonty and the Market Stance. They provided the street lighting by gas and paraffin. From 1892 - 1948 they organised a Fire Brigade. They employed a Town Crier.

In 1923 the Town Councils of Insch and Rothney united. The new provost wore the Insch chain and the Baron Bailie the Rothney chain. They saw to the upkeep of the playing fields and the children's play area. For a number of years they supported the Pipe Band. They cleaned the Valentine Burn. And they all had a good time at the Burghers Supper. All this and more until each responsibility in turn was taken over by local government. During its 117 years, the organisations using the hall have changed as the lifestyle of the people of Insch has changed.

The next building on the left is the Fordyce Hall where the Christian Brethren have been meeting for nearly 100 years.

The double house on the left, which you will recognise from this

Commerce Street, Insch
Photograph by Farquhar, Chemist.

Given to me by Miss Bella Horne.

photograph, was the former police station.

On the right St. Droston's Episcopal Church built in 1895. The house next door was formerly the Rectory.

Walk on to the cross roads. You have been walking along Gallows Road. Do not be alarmed, it has been known as Commerce Street for a long time. The gentle incline on Charles Street was the Gallows Hill.

From the 1842 Statistical Account "there is some probability that Insch, though but a burgh of barony, had had the power of pot and gallows". "Pot" meaning a deep hole dug in the ground, a pit, also applied to a natural pit or hollow in a rock etc. — a grisly form of punishment it seems.

Charles Street and Rannes Street, opposite, are names associated with Leith Hall. Look up Charles Street to the third house on the left. In the late 1920s Mr. Harvey, retired schoolmaster from Culsalmond and latterly Oyne, came to live here. While in Culsalmond he had taught classes of twenty to thirty young people to play the violin. After retiring to Insch he formed a West Church Orchestra comprising members of that church.

Later Provost John Anderson became conductor. Practises were held in his home, Insch-Home, Alexander Street and the orchestra was no longer entirely associated with the church.

It was in 1943, during Mr. Andersons's term as provost, that the 1565 Burgh of Barony Charter, by chance, came to light in H.M. General Register House, Edinburgh.

About 1927 Insch Melody Makers, a dance band was formed by Messrs. Danny Anderson, fiddle, Bob Bandeen

(who was church organist), piano, Harris Butchart, saxaphone and Jim Glennie, drums. The band continued into the 1930s with some changes of members.

In those days dances began at 8.00 pm and lasted through to 2.00 am with only two short breaks of about a quarter of an hour.

Mr. Harris Butchart is a third generation merchant of Insch, now retired.

Many years later Mr. Bob Bandeen was appointed an Honorary Fellow of the Royal Society of Antiquarians for his work on local history in Strichen.

The Grant Family Dance Band is remembered by generations of Insch folk. It all began in 1906 when young Archibald Grant set off from Forgue on his bicycle with his trumpet strapped to his back, accompanied by the young lady pianist, also on bicycle, to play in the neighbouring village halls. All village halls had a piano, fortunately.

The young couple married and moved to live near Insch, acquired a motor-bike and side car with which they travelled to dances. They were joined by Mr. Alec Robertson on fiddle and became a three piece band and then by Mr. Don Middleton on drums. When their son and daughter grew up they also joined the band. For a time too, they had Mr. Willie Moir on fiddle.

In the late 1920s and through until the war Grant's Band played at picnics. Each district had its own picnic and sports day. The band performed on a horse-drawn lorry with a canopy. During the afternoon they played for Highland Dancing displays and afterwards, until it became dark, they played for general dancing. The band continued from 1906, through two wars until 1974. Mrs.

Grant retired at the age of eighty. She had been a member since she was thirteen years old.

To the west of Charles Street was the Village Lands where villagers rented grazing from the Laird of Leith Hall. Somerset Crescent now stands on part of those lands. Somerset, because a builder from that English county started the housing development here.

Before you turn left into Rannes Street pause to look at the ironmonger, plumber and undertaker firms of John Souter Ltd. The name over the original shop door was James Souter. The brothers had come from Rhynie about 1900 and when James died John took over the shop to add to his timber and joinery business. In 1928 at a very young age Gordon, his son, found himself head of the firm. He expanded into the building trade which lasted until 1980.

During the years 1949 - 1959 Mr. Gordon Souter was Provost of Insch and Rothney Town Council, progressing there too, particularly in the development of the playing fields and children's play area.

Rannes Street

THE first road on the left off Rannes Street is George Street but was more often called the Sa'mill road. It was here, in 1900, that John Souter built his sawmill which was in production until 1980 supplying many local needs and timber for coal mines.

Close by was his electric power station, built in 1913, which for 23 years supplied over 100 consumers in the village with electric light. The plant was closed in 1936 when the Grampian Electricity Supply Company took over.

On your right is the building known as The Institute which was opened in 1929. It was erected and endowed by Dr. John Russell O.B.E. in memory of his father, Mr. John Russell J.P. who founded the merchant business John Russell & Son. He also bequeathed his library and gave the bowling green.

In 1929, the first green keeper, the late Mr. George Williams, cut the grass with a scythe. He was soon to get a mower and remained for 20 years as caretaker of the grounds and premises including the snooker table. Insch Bowling Club Triples Cup was donated in his memory by his son. Two players who have won awards outwith the Club are Ian Laird and Michael Mennie.

When the Insch library became the responsibility of local government many of Dr. Russell's finest books were removed to Aberdeen libraries for safekeeping. First editions were replaced by later editions. It is still possible to borrow some of his books. He and the author Arnold Bennett were friends. The character Dr. Stirling in Bennett's novel "An Old Wives Tale" is based on the real life character of Dr. John Russell.

There is a photograph of Mr. John Russell J.P. in the library. On the walls of the reading room you will find a copy of Rob Roy's pass to Insch, signed by the Earl of Mar, in 1715 and photographs of some former provosts of the burgh. You could stop to read Mrs. Margaret Scott's book "Insch" — her impressions of the village. Miss J. Jaffrey, who latterly lived in Western Road, wrote her life story under the name J.A. Gordon.

Rob Roy's Pass to Insch
John, Earl of Mar General and Commander in Chief
of His Majestys Forces in Scotland to the Officers
Civil and Military and to the well-disposed subjects of
our Gracious Soverign King James the Eighth and all
others his Majestys subjects whom it concerns. Permit
the bearer hereof Robert Roy Campbell and his
servants ten in number freely to pass from this place to
Inch in Aberdeen upon his own lawful Business
giving him all manner of assistance both in going
thence and returning att his own Charges. Given from
the Camp at Pearth this eight of November.

1715   *Mar*

Walk on to Insch War Memorial Hospital. From a newspaper cutting dated 1922 "To perpetuate the memory of men from their districts who fell in the war the people of Insch and the neighbouring parishes of Premnay, Leslie, Culsalmond, Oyne and Chapel of Garioch have erected a handsome and splendidly equipped memorial hospital".

When the building of the ten bed hospital was proposed, it was estimated that the running cost would be £301.

In the entrance hall there are plaques with the names of people with Insch connections, living all over the world, who left legacies and gave donations for the building of the hospital. There is an oak tablet with the names of the fallen from the 1914 - 18 war and the 1939 - 45 war. There is a tablet, too, to the memory of Dr. George Mitchell 1909 - 52, general practitioner and surgeon of this hospital from its beginning until he died in 1952.

Fifty years later the people of Insch and districts added the day room to the original building.

In its 64 years Insch Hospital has only had three matrons.

In a "Britain in Bloom" competition of 1981, the Royal British Legion of Scotland awarded Insch Hospital and grounds the prize for the "Best Kept War Memorial". As you leave the grounds admire the fine boundary wall and remember Lizzie Green, housekeeper to Provost Martin, whose legacy financed its building.

The house on the corner, opposite the hospital gate, is Rannes Green built by Mr. & Mrs. George Glennie. He was the master slater who slated the roof of the church in Western Road in 1883. His nephew, also George Glennie, a master slater carried on his business. He had five sons who became slaters. This house was, for a time, the school house of Insch.

The Premnay Bed.

D'ye hear a' that noise like the trámplin' o' feet?
That's the fowk tae the Premnay Bazaar.
There's ane at Auchleven—anither at Insch,
An' they're croodin' frae near an' frae far.

Ye wint a' the story afore ye'll lench oot?
Ah weel, I believe that's but fair.
Ye mind o' the War, whaur sae mony lads fell,
As they focht—some on land—some in air?

Weel, we've biggit an Hospital, ower i' the Toon,
A model o' a' that is braw,
Tae the mem'ry o' them that gaed oot frae our midst,
An' we're needin' mair Siller! That's a'!

We want tae endow a sma' bed o' our ain,
An' it only tak's sax hunner poun';
You can mak' it a thousan', we winna' cry oot,
An your praise will be sung wi' renown.

When the Hospital's opened, an' suff'rin' relieved,
Ye'll think o' the graves ower the sea;
An' ye'll hear in the gloamin' a whisper sae sweet—
"Inasmuch!—Ye have done it to Me."

A. E. W.

Insch, 20th June, 1922.

This poem, by Mrs. A. Wallace, was sold and printed on a card to raise money for a Premnay bed.

Going towards Commercial Road

RETRACE your steps up Rannes Street and turn left at the top. Walk on until you come to the Shevock Burn and stand on the Bridge of Rothney. Until 1923 the towns each had their own provost and council. There was a friendly rivalry between the two villages. Rothney folk used to remark to each other that they were "gan ower Insch" when they intended crossing the bridge into Insch.

Stay by the bridge a little longer. There was a mill in Insch when Mary Queen of Scots granted her charter in 1565. The 1696 Poll Book tells us that there was a "Milne of Insch", John Sharp was the miller and there were Meldrums, Betties and Glennys living here then.

14th September 1919

SALE OF WORK

*Organised by the LARGIE BRANCH of the
ONWARD AND UPWARD ASSOCIATION*

IN AID OF THE

INSCH WAR MEMORIAL.

Poem by Mr LEITH HAY.

The little cot all spotless white
Is ready for the suffering child,
And in the ward, with flowers bright,
A picture hangs, "Our Saviour Mild."

The little one is carried in
With gentle hands and soothing touch
She sighs, and whispers soft and low—
"I'm comfy now, thanks, oh so much.

With tender care she's well at last,
The Doctor and the Nurse have won,
And anxious thoughts of parents past,
Who bless them both for what they've done.

And now, kind Friends, we're here to-day
To help the cause—"The Hospital."
For funds are needed still they say,
So please let's all be liberal,

And add some hundreds to the fund
To build what will to us recall
The gallant men who never shunned
Their duty, but bravely gave their all.

No doubt we've many calls to meet,
But this is one for which we must
Do all we can, so now I trust
The drawings here will be a treat.

Let everything be bought ere night,
And send our Friends from Bonnie Largie
Back home to dream of visions bright;
So spend, and mind no "argie bargie."

But ere we part we're going to hear
A play that sets most tongues a wagging,
A concert with sweet voices clear
Will charm us first, and then comes "Nagging."

Looking back to Commerce Street, the husk mill is on your left. If you walk up the burn side you will see the remains of the mill lade and the aqueduct which brought the water down to turn the wheels of the husk and corn mills. The axle of the wheel is still on the wall.

Across the street is the building which belongs to the plant hire firm of G. & R. Young. To remind us all that it once was a meal mill, the grinding stones have been incorporated in the wall facing the street. If you look down the side next to the burn you can see a fragment of the mill wheel on the wall. Some of the older people in Insch have told me that one of their earliest memories is that of being lifted from their beds by their parents and taken to see the corn mill burning. That was in 1919.

Walking up Commercial Road you will see a sign, "Mary Jane House". Mrs. Mary King Simpson, the artist who painted many local scenes, lived here. Mary Jane was the wife of the first owner.

A shed behind Anderson's shop and house was the home of the early fire engines. At first the vehicle was horse-drawn, that is except on a Monday, when should the need arise, a visiting dentist who hired a room at the shop would attach the appliance to his car.

In Commercial Road there are some houses which are built as two flats with a stone stair on the outside, at the back leading to the upper flat. There were many houses built in this style in Insch at one time. Many of the older houses were roofed with slates from the quarries on the Foudland hills.

A little further on, on the left, you will come to a house which stands very close indeed to its neighbour. This building was once a temperance hotel.

Before the coming of the railway a coach left the turnpike road leading through the Rothney lands and taking the road through Insch and returning to the Longford Bridge.

Annual horse fairs continued to be held well into this century. Horses arrived by train and were walked through the streets on their way to St. Sairs, Colpy. They were accompanied by "melodian johnnies" from Aberdeen who played in the streets; the bairns were handed round sweeties and some of the fun of the fair was enjoyed in the

This photograph was taken in the 1920s after the mill had been rebuilt.
The photographer, Mr. James Riddoch, was Provost of Insch and Rothney from 1945 - 49. The mills ceased to operate about 1964.

Station Hotel and the Rothney Fountain with Dunnydeer in the background.
Given to me by Miss B. Horne.

villages of Insch and Rothney. Horse-drawn brakes were provided by the Commercial Hotel for the lucky folk who could go all the way to St. Sairs.

Walk to the end of Commercial Road and look over to the Rothney Arms, previously known as the Station Hotel and built in the 1870s. (Earlier there had been a Rothney Inn.) For many years the hotel was owned and run by the McCombie family. Mrs. Jane McCombie came to the hotel in 1920, with her husband, and at the age of seventy became cook-in-charge. She died aged ninety-seven, Britain's oldest woman hotel licensee.

An advertisement from about 1930 states that the hotel "Boots attends all trains". "Commercial gentlemen" arrived by rail with their skips (hampers) and called on the village shops. They then hired a car with "an experienced chauffeur" and drove round the country shops, sometimes travelling as far as Wick and Thurso. If you wanted to telephone the hotel, the number was 3.

Weddings were catered for in the hotel. Dinner dances were catered for in the public hall which meant transporting all that was required, and outside catering for a roup (farm sale) literally took place outside on an open fire enclosed by bricks over which a metal frame was placed to support the large cooking pots. Tables were laid with cloths, cutlery, glasses and china in the barn and a three-course lunch was served and later a high tea. All this plus the staff having been transported from Insch in the hotel's well scrubbed cattle float. Sometimes a roup lasted for more than one day.

The north wing of the hotel, now greatly altered, was once the stables and coach house. Visitors to Insch could stable their horses here. During World War II the buildings were converted to shower and bathrooms for the troops, billeted in the district.

Between the railway station and the hotel stands the Rothney Fountain, erected by Rothney Town Council in 1893. The pillar is of Corrennie granite and the spire is of Kemnay granite. The inauguration ceremony, which took place in the late afternoon of a dark winters' day, was performed by Miss Gordon of Newton. There was a circle of torch bearers round the fountain and the windows of Provost Beaton's Station Hotel were brilliantly lit. Children of Insch and Rothney who had gathered round the fountain were presented with fruit by members of the Council. In his speech Town Clerk Wallace said the Council's original idea arose from a wish to provide water for the tired and thirsty beasts but they had now provided water for man and beast.

A large crowd of people on their way home from the Upper Garioch Champion ploughing match, which had been held at Ladywell, joined the local people round the fountain. Competitors had travelled from as far as Caithness to take part in the match.

You have now reached a very important place in the village of Rothney. The date on the Railway Station is 1880 but this is the second station. The earlier wooden station was built in 1854 at the time the line came through from Kittybrewster to Huntly. The coming of the railway brought prosperity to the villages of Insch and Rothney. The Station "Maister" was a man of standing in the community. Sometimes several members of one family were employed

Right: Mr. Laidlaw Smith, the master, and Mr. Wm. Metcalfe, the huntsman, with the pack at the Aberdeenshire Riding Club's first drag hunt at Insch.
Picture courtesy of "The People's Journal".

On the corner opposite the Station Hotel, by Wallace's shop in 1933.
Loaned by Miss Thelma Smith.

on the railway as were the father and four sons of the Milne family, Railway Cottage, Dias.

A day trip to Aberdeen by train, even well into this century, was for some people, children in particular, an event likely to occur only once or twice a year. It was an adventure for which careful preparations had to be made. "Sunday" or best clothes were carefully laid out on the previous evening so that there would be a perfect start on the great day.

There were many stops on the way in those days but not for a "swifty". That was an express train and you would not have been able to take one from Insch. Insch Station has won several prizes over its one hundred years for gardens and cleanliness etc., six of these are framed and hung on the walls of the waiting room. Individual members of staff also won prizes.

There are many railway stories. One day the level crossing gates (not the present ones), had swung slightly ajar in a strong wind. A puzzled motorist stopped his car and called up to the signal-man asking him to explain what he meant by having the gates half open. "Well", said the signal-man, "we are half expecting a train".

Gordon Terrace

As you leave the station turn right into Gordon Terrace. Pause on the pavement. The Station Master used to live in the house on your right.

Look across the street. Town Clerk Wallace had his merchant business in the premises on the corner. He and his family lived in the house which you are now facing. His wife Mrs. Annie Wallace was for twenty years an invalid. She wrote poems, one of which was set to music by Mr. Fowlie, piano teacher at Insch School. And one "The Premnay Bed" was sold, printed on a card, to raise funds to provide a Premnay bed for Insch War Memorial Hospital.

If you had come here on a summers' evening it is possible that you would have found the Choral Union singing a few choruses for Mrs. Wallace before their conductor, Mr. George Innes, caught the train for Aberdeen. Mr. Innes was also the conductor of the Hall Russell Male Voice Choir. The Choral Union's first conductor was Mr. John Robertson, Muiryheadless. All the

Committee of the Insch Choral Society.
Left to right (ladies): *Miss Mennie, Miss C. Stewart (accompanist), Mrs Cruickshank, Misses Smith and Anderson (joint secretaries).*
Gentlemen: *Messrs A.A. McIntosh, J. Anderson (treasurer), J. Wallace (vice-president), and D.M. Robertson (president).*
Inset: *Mr George A. Innes, Aberdeen (conductor).*
(Mr. Adam McIntosh was a shoemaker and a Rothney "character".)

Robertson Family were involved in the choir as were the Grassick Family, Sleepytoon and the Thomson Family, Chapelton. Members came from Oyne, Culsalmond, Leslie and Premnay. Leslie folk walked down to attend practises when the weather was too bad for them to cycle.

Mr. P. Reid, music teacher at Insch School was conductor for a time. The Choral Union lasted through the 1920s into the early 1930s and was fifty to sixty strong. Included in their repertoire was Hiawatha and The Messiah. On one occasion in Aberdeen, they won a shield as the best choir in the North East in a competition.

I talked to four ex-choir members living in Insch, Mrs. M. Macfarlane, Mr. P. Russell, Mr. H. Thomson and Mrs. I. Young. They recalled the joy they experienced singing with the Choral Union.

About this time, too, Mr. Willie Milne, a clerk at the Station was a well known fiddler. In the late 1930s he taught fiddle music in evening classes at Insch School. Some years later a station master, Mr. Cruickshank formed a Reel and Strathspey Society.

There were so many people involved in musical societies in Insch that it would be impossible to name them all. It was said that Insch housewives "stirred the porridge to the runs of the Hallelujah Chorus".

Walk down Gordon Terrace. In one of the houses on the left, before you reach the mart, Mr. James Horne celebrated his hundredth birthday, app-

House in Gordon Terrace in earlier times. Note the street water supply to the left of the photograph.
Loaned by Mrs O. Ritchie.

ropriately on Saint Valentine's Day, 1968.

Until fairly recently, Rothney was a town quite separate from Insch. Births, marriages and deaths were registered in the Parish of Premnay and Premnay rates were paid. The only building which bore the name Insch was the Station. Rothney peoples' daily requirements were provided for within their town. Their daily paper delivery was organised from the Station.

From morning until she retired to bed, Mrs. Park's shop was open, her shelves stocked with a miscellany of goods. Towards the end of the 1939 - 45 war Parkie grew old and stiff. Sweetie coupons and points became more and more troublesome and her stock dwindled. In an evening when the shop bell tinkled while she was seated by her fire, she would call out, "Nae ciggies, nae sweeties and sweet damn aal". Mrs. Park's shop is no more in Gordon Terrace. The building was for a time the Gordon Terrace Cafe. The outline of its position can still be seen on one of the houses.

The mart was founded by Central & Northern Farmers Co-op Society Ltd. about 1900. No longer were cattle sold in the open on Market Mere.

For a moment, turn your back on the Mart and look over in the direction of the railway line. Although cattle were walked from the farm to the mart they made their last journey by rail to the slaughter house. As the sale progressed the cattle made their way to the empty trucks waiting for them in the goods yard opposite. On a busy day as many as 44 trucks with 10 cattle to a truck would leave for the south, some going to England.

Seed potatoes went south by rail, too, and straw for the paper mills in Fife. Arriving from the south, goods vehicles containing grain for the milling company, cattle feed, fertilisers and coal were driven into a siding to be off-loaded and taken away by carrier. Groceries and furniture for the local shops were off-loaded in a shed.

The mart premises have been extended several times and are now owned by Aberdeen and Northern Marts.

Next to the dwelling house on the right is an open yard. Through the 1920s to 1935 this place was a hive of activity. Mr. William Reid, a self-taught, inventive engineer, owned seven travelling threshing mills. Each mill had its steam engine and caravan with sleeping accommodation for the team of men who operated the mill. They travelled to farms in the surrounding countryside, to Alford, Kildrummy, Lumsden, Culsalmond and as far as Glenlivet. The men fed in the farm house along with all the extra hands that were needed on the day that the "stem-mull" came. In the yard in Insch there was a large work-shop where the engines and mills were repaired and maintained.

Walk to the last two houses in the street which stand opposite each other, Oldtown of Rothney, birthplace of Mr. Alexander Wilson in 1780 (see High Street — "The Life of Alexander Wilson"). The family dwelling-house was on one side of the street and the carpentry work shop on the other.

Walk beyond the houses and look over to the railway line again. A little to this side of the underpass there used to be a small hut. It was from there that the Aberdeen express train collected the mail. A postman suspended the mail bag

Dunnydeer from Insch.
Given to me by Miss B. Horne.

from an iron gantry in a precisely calculated position. As the express came down the line the mail was caught in a net.

Turn to face the opposite direction. The hill to the south behind the Station is sometimes called the Carrier's Hill by local people but you will find it marked Rothney Hill, 652 feet, on Ordnance Survey maps.

Some of the early views of Insch were photographed from the hill which gives them a bird's eye view effect.

If you have time and the weather is fine walk back to Charles Street and turn left at the top. Before you get to the Cemetery, on the left is the Old (Established Church) Manse built in 1771. Carry on past the Smiddy until you come to a bend in the road. Look up

now to Dunnydeer which "catches the eye of the stranger at a great distance" (from my old friend the 1842 Statistical Account). Insch people are proud of their connections with this famous place.

The hill is 876 feet high. What you see on the top is the remaining wall of the earliest tower-house on the Scottish mainland. It was built in the thirteenth century using vitrified stone from the fort within which it stands. Beyond the fort is an earthwork rampart with a ditch on either side. Dr. W. Douglas Simpson wrote, "The whole thus forms one of the most remarkable archaeological ensembles in the North of Scotland". Take a look at that.

I do hope you have enjoyed this walk around Insch. ₁

Insch in 1980s, photographed from Dunnydeer Hill.